FOR MY SON

A guided journal for a parent to record family and lifetime lessons to share with a son

May you always find the strength to face challenges with confidence in life's journey, and the compassion to stop to help someone along the way.

Copyright © by Kai-Nneka Townsend 2022
All rights reserved

THIS **JOURNAL** IS FOR

_____

_____

ABOUT THIS JOURNAL

For My Son is a great way to record your own family or life lessons to share with your son for keepsake, to cherish forever. The journal is filled with simple prompts and inspirational quotes to guide you along in your writing.

A FEW TIPS

- Complete the journal in any order – write as you feel inspired
- The prompts are there as a guide – but feel free to make them your own. Some blank pages have been included for you to write your own themes and include any mementos such as a photo or other keep-sake items
- Go at your own pace but do have a goal in mind for when you want to complete and gift to your son
- Choose your own style to record these family and lifetime lessons – you can tell stories about experiences, write a few quick lines down, include your own quotes, make it quirky or funny. Whatever you do, make it authentically you

ABOUT YOU

"You don't raise heroes, you raise sons. And if you treat them like sons, they'll turn out to be heroes, even if it's just in your own eyes"

Walter M. Schirra Sr.

First of all – I love you because...

I am proud of you because...

I wish for you...

LIFE

"Always hold your head up, but be careful to keep your nose at a friendly level"

Max L. Forman

"Every child is an artist. The problem is how to remain an artist once we grow up"

Pablo Picasso

Dream big, and protect your dreams...

"Never stop learning and adapting. The world will always be changing. If you limit yourself to what you knew and what you were comfortable with earlier in life, you will grow increasingly frustrated with your surroundings as you age."

David Niven

Your attitude will determine your altitude in life...

Life will come at you hard, but know this...

"Our greatest glory is not in never failing, but in rising up every time we fail."

Confucius

It's okay to make mistakes...

It's okay to choose a different path, than the one I dreamed for you…

"May you always be the one who sees the light in the little things"

Unknown

Always be thankful...

RELATIONSHIPS & LOVE

"When you fully trust someone without any doubt, you finally get one of two results:

- ★ A person for life or
- ★ A lesson for life

Unknown

"Find a group of people who will challenge and inspire you; spend a lot of time with them, and it will change your life."

Amy Poehler

Keep your friends close...

Choosing a partner...

Marriage isn't easy but...

"Even seasonal situations can bring with them lessons that last a lifetime. If the love doesn't last, it prepares you for the next one that will."

Mandy Hale

It may be time to let go of a friend or partner if...

Regardless of what happens, know that
I will be here for you...

MONEY & FINANCE

"The time to repair the roof is when the sun is shining"

John F. Kennedy

Have a financial plan for now, and for your future...

Think about investments...

Always choose good character over money...

CAREER & BUSINESS

"Some people want it to happen. Some wish it could happen. Others make it happen."

Michael Jordan

Your first career choice doesn't have to be your only career choice...

"To be yourself in a world that is constantly trying to make you something else is the greatest accomplishment."

Ralph Waldo Emerson

Don't be afraid to step out and be your own boss...

EDUCATION & LEARNING

"Other people's opinion of you does not have to become your reality."

Les Brown

Some of the best things I learned in school were...

FAMILY

"Life is ten percent what you experience and ninety percent how you respond to it."

Dorothy M. Neddermeyer

As a family we have learned…

Here's what you should know about me...

Here's what you should know about your grandparents...

And another thing...

FOR KEEPSAKE

"The man who moves a mountain begins by carrying away small stones"

Confucius

I thought you should also know that...

Always remember that *I love you*

Always remember that *I love you*

Always remember that *I love you*

Always remember that *I love you*

Always remember that *I love you*

Always remember that *I love you*

Always remember that *I love you*

Always remember that *I love you*

Always remember that *I love you*

Always remember that *I love you*

I thought you may also want to cherish these things, to remember how much I love you.

Always remember that *I love you*

Always remember that *I love you*

Always remember that *I love you*

Always remember that *I love you*

Always remember that *I love you*

Always remember that *I love you*

Always remember that *I love you*

Always remember that *I love you*

Always remember that *I love you*

Always remember that *I love you*

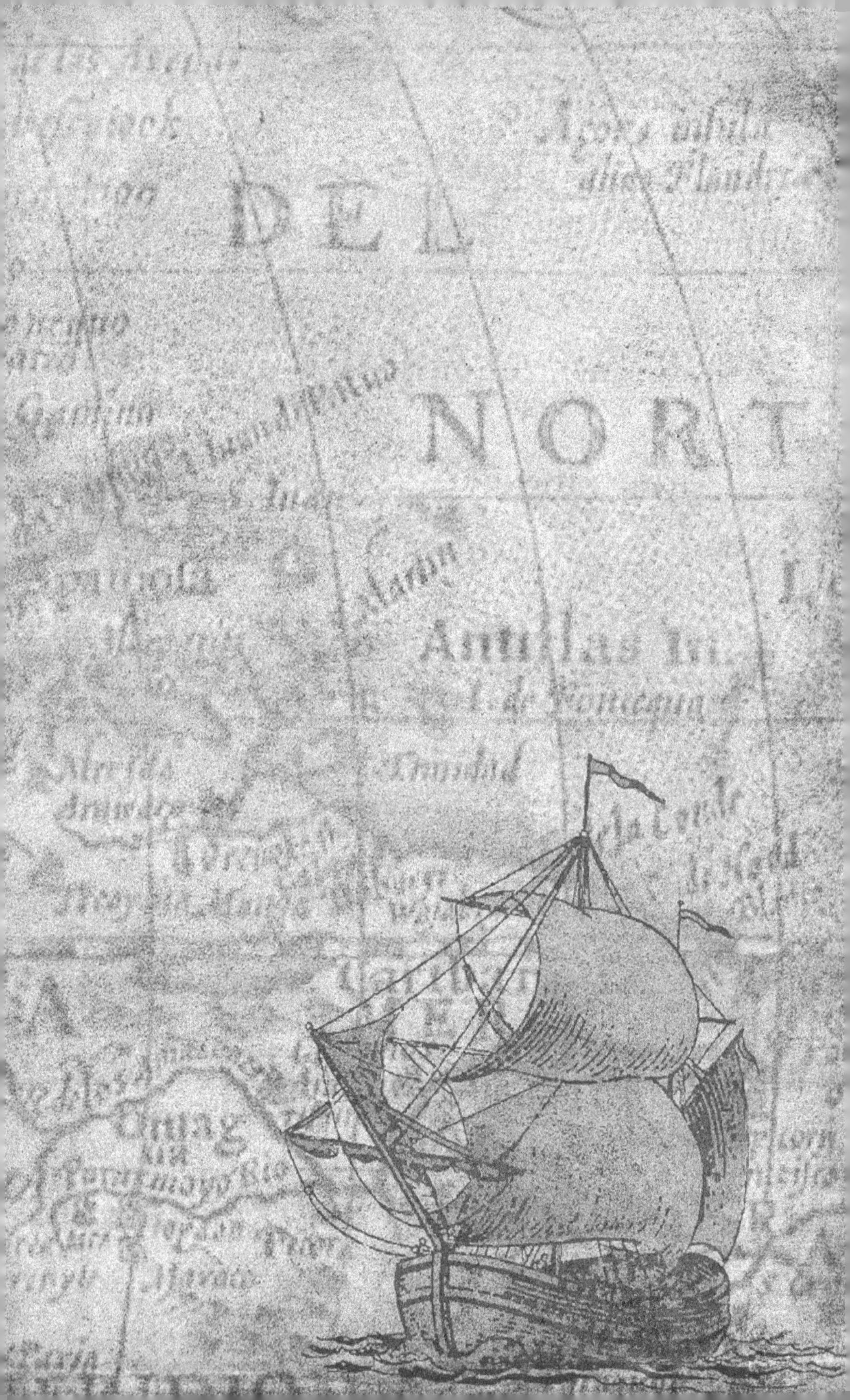
DEL
NORT